Chasing Hemingway

Five Journeys on My Way to Here

Rick McAllister

Chasing Hemingway
Five Journeys on My Way to Here

Copyright, 2020
Rick McAllister

No text or images in this book
may be used or reproduced in any
manner without written permission
of the copyright holders.

All Rights Reserved

Cover layout and interior pages
layout by Capri Porter.

Printed in the United States of America

ISBN: 978-1-7322135-8-6

Published by
Legacies & Memories
St. Augustine, Florida

www.LegaciesandMemoriesPublishing.com

Dedicated with Love to my Granddaughters:

McAllister Claire Whelan

and

Lucy Malone Whelan

Contents

Dedication

Introduction

First Journey: Vespa...15

Second Journey: War...28

Third Journey: The Florida Keys...44

Forth Journey: Cuba...57

Fifth Journey: Spain...70

Epilogue...87

Quotation Sources...89

Bibliography...91

About the Author...93

Introduction

A couple years ago, a friend invited me to speak to the men's club at his country club. While I was honored to be invited, I wasn't sure what I would speak about. For a number of years, I had done quite a few presentations throughout the Southeastern United States, but all were centered on two topics: my black and white photographic gallery exhibit titled *The Olde South Series*, and the 500 mile walk across Northern Spain on the Camino de Santiago which I have done three times. These were easy to present, and I had plenty of photographic support for fill-in, but I didn't think these were what fifty, financially comfortable, sporting men would want to listen to while they sipped their favorite cocktail.

Pondering this for several days, one of my golfing buddies suggested sharing with them some of the special events that I have experienced. Every Wednesday I have entertained them with anecdotes and snippets from some of these journeys, mostly at the 19th hole, and for one reason or another, they found them at least slightly entertaining. Perhaps it was just the beer.

So that's what I did. I took five events in my life that I felt were not only instrumental in shaping who Rick McAllister really is but events that also had some special moments within them that perhaps set them apart from similar journeys taken by others. That later point I don't think is really that important because the real issue is the impact they had on me at that particular time of my life. These five events are the basis for the five chapters in this book.

As I started to formulate my thoughts around these events and made some notes which would lead to an outline and eventually a draft of my talk, I noticed an odd quirk. All five of them had a connection or a link to my favorite writer and author, Ernest Hemingway. I didn't plan it that way. As a matter of fact, the thought never came into my mind until I started to outline my first journey and the connection to what I consider his best work, *The Old Man and the Sea*.

The Old Man and the Sea was the second book I ever read, the first being *Call of the Wild* by Jack London. Both books had been given to me by my father when I was around 13 or 14 years old in an attempt to interest me in something other than sports and girls. At the time, I don't think it really worked because reading and good study habits never really kicked in until my sophomore year in college, and then only under the duress of limited options. But, that little book about an old Cuban fisherman pitting his aging physical and emotional capabilities against a very large marlin and against mother nature herself resonated with me and remained tucked away in my psyche until much later in my life when other Hemingway references would brush against me.

As the title might suggest, I haven't really been chasing Hemingway in some diabolical or nefarious manner. As a young adult in my 30s, I started reading a few more of his novels and short stories, which in turn whet an appetite to learn a little more about this bigger than life persona who, as I had discovered, had some pretty wild adventures, both socially and in the field. For one thing there is no doubt that he is one of the great American authors. There is also little doubt about another: that while his life was full of these manly pursuits like fishing and hunting and bullfights, his personal life took on a more tumultuous life of its own. Drinking and womanizing woven throughout his four marriages, combined with his narcissism and dark moods, lead to an observation made by Pulitzer prize winning novelist William Kennedy who wrote of Hemingway in the *New*

York Times, that he presented a "complex and profoundly dramatic story of a man's extraordinary effort to stay alive."

America has always opened its arms to heroes, particularly those who exhibited bravery in their heroic actions. Hemingway was attracted to bravery, and while he exhibited it during his military service and during his years of war reporting, later in life he liked associating with those who had earned a public acknowledgement of bravery as if it elevated his own aging masculinity which was declining for a variety of reasons. Men who exhibited courage and bravery also became the main characters in his writings; Santiago in *The Old Man and the Sea*, Robert Jordon in *For Whom the Bell Tolls*, Jake Barnes in *The Sun Also Rises*, and Thomas Hudson in *Islands in the Stream*.

I like Ernest Hemingway for the spirit with which he tackled his passions. We liked the same things; fishing, boating, baseball, outdoor adventures and travel, writing and women. We spent time and had connections with the same places: Spain, The Florida Keys, Cuba, and the American West. We even shared some of the same demons although the manner in which we acknowledged them and accepted them was dramatically different. Ernest let his get the better of him in 1961 when he took his own life in Idaho. It is these connections and that spirit that, to this day, stimulate me to continue to trace his journeys and that inspires me to still "chase Hemingway."

Chasing Hemingway

Five Journeys
on My Way to Here

First Journey: Vespa 1959

"Every day is a new day."
Ernest Hemingway

Every kid, at one time or another, has said "I'm going to run away." They then jump on their bicycle and make it to the end of the street before the big question pops into their fledgling minds, "where in the hell am I going to go, and what will I do when I get there?" So they turn around, ride home, chew a little crow, and continue the day as if nothing happened. I took a bit of a different approach.

Christmas morning 1959 was perhaps the most exciting Christmas I have ever had. Sitting next to the tree that Mom so meticulously decorated a few nights before was a brand new, baby blue Allstate Cruisaire motor scooter (a Vespa motor scooter manufactured by Piaggio and distributed in the United States by Sears). I had some casual conversations with my Dad about scooters and mopeds (in Ohio you could ride a motorbike that had less than 5 horsepower at the age of 14) but nothing really led me to believe that I would actually get one. But there it was.

My world expanded significantly with independent means of transportation, and Dixie Gunther (who had a Cushman Eagle scooter) and I were the only two at school at that age who were not dependent upon their parents or older kids for a ride. It was pretty cool and life as a fourteen-year-old was getting cooler by the minute. I already was a noted athlete in baseball and swimming and this year added football to my resume. In the Cincinnati high school system, fraternities and sororities were sanctioned and very active, and I was in BOA (the one the girls thought was the coolest and the one that all the jocks belonged to). However, all this peripheral activity took a toll on my grades, not that they were ever very strong, and then the hammer dropped. Mom and Dad said that if I got anything less than a "C" on my report card, I would no longer be allowed to play football and I would have to quit the fraternity. My sister Sharon, 11 months younger than me, was the brain of the McAllister clan. She could handle sorority life, take piano lessons, and still achieve family acclaim with her report card. I, on the other hand, placed studying somewhere significantly below sports, girls and just about all else that floats in front of teenage boys. This was a disaster at its worst as I knew I was getting something less than a "C" in chemistry. What would I do and how could I face my friends, particularly after flaunting my very naive good fortune.

In my mind there was only one solution: run away from home. I mean really run away and with the scooter, I certainly had the means to go further than the candy store at the end of our street. So I planned my trip. Every summer we vacationed in Fort Lauderdale, Florida, a 1,200+ mile trip from Cincinnati, but it was the only location and direction that popped into my spinning head. After a couple days of lackadaisical planning, I told my sister of my plans and swore her to secrecy. On Monday morning, the day the report cards were due out, and on the morning that my dad would be driving the car pool, I grabbed my jacket and books and told Dad that I would wait in the garage. My Vespa was packed with one change of underwear, an extra shirt, a small book, and I had $38.00 in my pocket.

When I opened the garage door, it was pouring down rain, it was chilly, it was the last week of October, and not an ideal day for going anywhere on two wheels. In my mind I was committed so I kick started the scooter, zipped up my non-waterproof jacket and off I went, hoping to be quiet enough so as to not alert parental curiosity in the kitchen on the other side of the garage wall.

During the first few miles, I probably had second thoughts about the stupidity of this plan, but nevertheless, I continued. In 30 minutes or so I was at the Ohio River ready to cross into Kentucky, the second state that I would journey through, and I was soaked. In another 20 minutes I was through Covington and needed to get out of the rain so I pulled into an old gas station/truck stop type of place. My jacket had some kind of fleece lining and it was soaked through to the core, so I took it off and laid it across one of those old fashioned type cast iron heaters that pumped hot water through them and always seemed to make those weird crackling sounds. Not only did this dry my jacket but caused the lining to catch fire. When I finally got it out, the entire inside of the jacket was a scorched mess and it smelled. The adventure was just beginning.

That first day I traveled 170 miles, arriving in Corbin, Kentucky for the evening (for you trivia buffs, Corbin is the home of Harlan Sanders, the founder of Kentucky Fried Chicken. On our trips to Ft. Lauderdale, we would stop the first morning and have breakfast at the restaurant associated with his motel, The Sanders

Motel). Now remember I left home with $38.00; after paying for a motel room, a package of cinnamon rolls for dinner, and going to the movie to see Kim Novak and Spencer Tracey in *Strangers When We Met*, I still had about $18.00 left. Still no thoughts about turning around.

Tuesday morning the rain had stopped but it was cold. Riding through the Southern hills of Kentucky and the mountains of Tennessee chilled me to the bone, but I was making good progress. Late in the afternoon, I was cruising about 50 mph into an area north of Atlanta when all of a sudden my accelerator stopped functioning; I could turn the handle but nothing happened as the engine continued to race at a high rpm. While I am not much of a mechanical person even to this day, I knew enough to shut the bike off and get safely to the side of the road. That I did, pulling into a roadside fruit and vegetable market. After a quick assessment I realized the throttle cable had broken.

This was about half-way into my journey and should have been a good time to reconsider what I was doing; I had lost my means of transportation and a clear mind should have said "enough is enough, go home." The key here being some kind of a clear thought process. Well, no garages appeared within site so I made a quick decision to lock the scooter behind the store and start walking while I tried to figure out a new plan to continue my travel Southward. After an hour or so, I was getting tired and needed to think about where I was going to spend the night. At the time, I happened to be standing on a sidewalk in front of a lot where they sold mobile homes. There were no cars around and the small office appeared to be closed for the evening. Is it possible that one of the models was left unlocked? It was worth a try so I started checking the doors on the models and sure enough, the second one I tried, the door opened. Guess where I spent the night? I climbed into the model and into the furnished bed and was sound asleep in no time (don't think I had anything to eat that night). I decided that in the morning I would start hitchhiking (keep in mind here that I had never once hitchhiked).

Wednesday started delightfully; the sun was out, the weather looked great, and the morning traffic was busy on whatever route it was that I was walking beside. It was a North/South route so it worked for me and it was time to try out this hitch hiking thing. Stood on the curb and put my thumb out; no big deal. Within five minutes, my chariot arrived.

It was a bright red Chevrolet Belair convertible with the top down – two guys appearing to be in their mid-twenties in the front seat. They asked me where I was going, I said "South," they said "Hop in" and off we went. I don't recall their names, but over the next few hours I learned that they both had washed out of the Army (I think for medical reasons) and they were on their way to the citrus area of Central Florida to pick oranges and grapefruit. They bought me a hamburger for lunch, didn't ask a lot of personal questions, and ultimately told me they were heading to the Tampa area. I had never been there but it was in Florida and that worked for me.

We pulled into the Tampa area about 9 p.m. and then I got the "Oh by the way. . . there is a curfew in Tampa for minors. . .none allowed on the streets after 8 p.m." Great, here I am in a town I've never been to before and not supposed to be out and about. They dropped me off in an industrial area which had a significant railroad presence. I ran over to one of the boxcars on a side rail that had its side door open, looked into the empty, dirty cavernous space and climbed in. Once again, I slept like a baby with no thought about what potentially bad circumstances I just put myself into.

Day three: I was on the West Coast of Florida and I needed to get to the East Coast of the state. Maybe there were trains that ran in that direction and perhaps I could jump one and "ride the rails." I followed one of the tracks that seemed to head East until I got into a wooded area where I wouldn't be noticed, and waited for the next train. Within a couple hours, I heard the distinctive sound of an approaching locomotive, and got ready for the next part of this adventure. Being true to my 14-year-old inexperienced self, I had no idea how fast these trains flew down the tracks; there was no way I could grab on let alone even reach any of the handles. The train rapidly passes and I am still in the middle of the woods with no idea where the nearest road is. The first doubts of the intelligence of this journey started to creep into my thoughts, but I couldn't stop here. Where was "here" anyway?

I followed the tracks knowing at some point they would intersect a road. A couple hours later that's exactly what happened and the old thumb came back out. So for the remainder of the day, I made my way from somewhere East of Tampa to Fort Lauderdale, climbing in and out of a dozen or so early day "Ubers," all of whom challenged my young threshold. As a family, we attended an Episcopal church every Sunday and for a couple pre-teen years, I was an acolyte carrying in the cross at the head of the choir. Cub Scouts, Boy Scouts. . .the whole nine yards of child and youth development. Apparently not enough of the street smarts stuff though because I wasn't prepared for my hitchhiking exposures.

There was a family of three who owned an A&W Root Beer Stand and wanted to adopt me (I think I looked like potential child labor); there was the gay guy who put his hand on my leg at a stoplight, whom I took a wild swing at, missed and jumped out of the car before the light could change; several girls who were the proverbial tease, and last but certainly not least, the semi- truck driver who stopped every 50 miles or so at a bar for a quick "pick me up." I met more of the world on that one day than I had in my previous sheltered 14 years.

I finally got to Fort. Lauderdale about 7 p.m. and I was tired. Not just sleepy tired but tired of my "adventure." It was about 70 degrees and I am walking through a resort area in my jeans and my burnt out winter jacket. Even I knew I looked out of place, and as I contemplated turning myself into the police, one of Fort Lauderdale's finest pulled up alongside the curb with his lights flashing. He asked me if I had some ID but before I could even pull my wallet out of my pocket, I told him I was Rick McAllister and that I recently ran away from my home in Cincinnati. To my utter amazement (although it should not have been) he said "I know. . .we have been expecting you." He politely put me into his cruiser and took me to the station.

While I don't remember all the procedures we went through once I arrived there, I do remember getting my picture taken and then being escorted to a small office where the officer asked if I was ready to go home. With tears welling up rapidly, I told him I was and he handed me the phone and made me call home. This call stands firm as perhaps the most difficult, yet soothing at the same time, calls I have ever made. My Dad answered the phone and all he said to me was "Are you ready to come home?" With a very embarrassed "yes" response, he then said he would be down the next day to get me.

Even though I eventually realized there weren't really any other options, I was placed in one of the cells and the door was locked with a clang I will never forget. I was finally in a safe haven yet I was scared to death. The officer asked if I wanted anything and I asked if I could have the book that I had been carrying the entire journey. He returned momentarily with *The Old Man and the Sea*, the book my Dad had given me several months before. I didn't really know who Ernest Hemingway was, but by the time my dad arrived the next day to pick me up, I had read the entire book. Funny, I had slept soundly in a strange motel, in an empty mobile home, and in a railroad car, but I couldn't catch a wink in that cell. After reading all that night, I think even at 14, I came away realizing that I would one day have a connection with the sea.

Dad took me to a hotel where I showered and got some decent food. We flew home from Fort Lauderdale to Cincinnati with long spurts of silence interrupted by fatherly questions. By the time I walked into our house and hugged my Mom, I fully realized how much pain I had inflicted upon them. My best friend told me that when he had called to check on why I wasn't in school, my Dad was crying. We all made it through this event and while it seemed to disappear from any family memories, it has remained to this day the first real steps in my life's journey. While the seeds of my life were planted early with a strong Christian childhood nurtured by my parents and my grandparents, those seeds were certainly fertilized by my "Vespa" adventure.

As a brief aside, when I turned 16, got my driver's license, and was engaged in conversations with my Dad about a car, I remember my Mom saying, "Look what he did at 14 with a motor scooter. What do you think we are looking at with a car?"

Addendum: I was allowed to continue playing

football and to remain a member of my fraternity. Dad drove down to Atlanta with a business associate, paid a fine, and picked up my motor scooter from the impound lot. Word eventually spread among my friends at school that I made it a little farther than the candy store at the end of the street... that was pretty cool.

Hemingway's "Old Man and the Sea" was written in 1951 in Cuba and published in 1952. It tells the story of an aging Cuban fisherman, Santiago, and his solitary fight with a very large marlin. For the longest period of time, Santiago as a fisherman was very unlucky, "salao," and even his young village friend, Manolin, was forbidden by his parents to fish with Santiago. At the end of these fruitless days, Manolin would help Santiago with his gear and they would talk of Joe DiMaggio and baseball. On the 85th day of his bad luck, Santiago hooks a huge marlin in the Gulf Stream and this begins a three-day struggle between "brothers." After this epic battle, the fish is brought and secured to the side of his boat and a new battle begins as he tries to protect his "brother" from marauding sharks. Perhaps his most *famous short novel, it won the Pulitzer Prize for Fiction in 1953 and was cited by the Nobel Committee as a significant reason for his Nobel Prize in Literature in 1954. Hemingway's Nobel prize was accepted in Stockholm by American Ambassador John C. Cabot as Hemingway was recovering from a couple plane crashes in Africa. After a review in Life magazine, "The Old Man and the Sea" sold 5 million copies in two days.*

Sitting on my Vespa in the same jacket
that caught on fire in Kentucky.

Second Journey: War 1969

*"Never think that war, no matter how necessary,
nor how justified, is not a crime. Ask the infantry
and ask the dead."*

Ernest Hemingway

What a decade the 60s were! As teenagers, we were inoculated daily with not only our own physiological and psychological growing pains, but the world was throwing stuff at us faster than most of us could absorb; hence the dramatic rise in strange substances to help us "absorb." The Cold War; the race in space and the landing on the moon; political scandals and assassinations; Woodstock and the music: the Beatles and the British invasion; and a brewing conflict in a little sliver of land that most Americans couldn't point to on a world map.

I graduated from high school in 1963 and from college in 1968 (yes for you math wizards it took me five years to get that blessed degree, but I got the damn thing even after my high school counselor told my parents don't bother sending your son to college . . .he's not college material). So while I grew up in the heart of this tumultuous time, I was pretty naive when it came to understanding not only the conflict in Vietnam itself, but the entire political quagmire that put us there in the first place and then kept us there until 58,000+ American men and women had been killed. I did understand, however, that when I received my Bachelor of Science degree from Susquehanna University in Selinsgrove, Pennsylvania in June of 1968, I was prime bait for the military draft.

Through the college placement program, I had accepted a management training program with The Equitable Life Assurance Society. Four of my fraternity brothers had accepted positions with this insurance giant as well, and we were all assigned field offices to complete our training. I was off to Syracuse.

Within 30 days of leaving the nest and taking the world on by myself, I received the infamous "greeting" letter from Uncle Sam along with a notice that my draft status had changed from "1-S" (student) to "1-A" (Available for military service). I knew it was coming and I was prepared to serve my country, as my family had done in the past. My grandfather was in World War

I with the Army Corps of Engineers in France, and my dad was a decorated Marine pilot in the South Pacific during World War II.

Several days later I received notice of my scheduled date for my physical exam. My original selective service branch was in Cincinnati. However, since I was now in Syracuse, I changed my branch to the Syracuse unit and that delayed the whole draft process for me by at least six months. Once the paperwork caught up with me, I passed my physical with flying colors and was sworn in on September 12, 1969. I should point out that I got married 22 days before going off to war.

I took my basic training at Fort Dix in New Jersey and my AIT (Advanced Individual Training) at Fort Lewis near Seattle, Washington. I had several offers to go off to officers candidate school (both from the Army and from the Navy) but since I had a good job waiting for me when I got out, I opted for the shortest military commitment which was the draft (two years active duty, two years active reserve, and two years inactive reserves).

Even though I was a college graduate and had actually started my Master's program, I ended up with an infantry MOS. (For the longest time I couldn't understand why the Army wouldn't want to use my education in a more efficient manner. This was not my only lack of early on understanding of the military ways.)

After completing the 10-week AIT program at Fort Lewis, I was given seven days leave before I was to ship out with orders to report to the Republic of South Vietnam. After our short respite in San Francisco, I drew my jungle fatigues and left from Travis Air Force Base in Oakland. We refueled in Anchorage, in Guam, and again in Yokota, Japan before ultimately arriving at Tan Son Nhut Air Base in the Republic of South Vietnam. My world would never be the same from this moment on.

I arrived a PFC and after a couple days waiting for a unit assignment, I received orders to join the 101st Airborne Division in I Corps (the Northern most corps in South Vietnam). A dozen of us or so were put on a C130 and transported to Phu Bai where we joined the "Screaming Eagles" and spent seven days going through their "P Training" where we were given an overview of what was in store for the next 12 months: Simulated patrols through controlled villages and rice fields, as well as presentations on the type of enemy troops and activity we could expect. It was going to be a long year and we were told that 25% of us would go home in a body bag.

I was assigned to Company E, 1/502nd Infantry (1st Battalion, 2nd Regiment). Our motto was "STRIKE – I fight where I am told and I win where I fight". Upon arriving at Company headquarters in Phu Bai, I drew my equipment (M16, ammo, backpack, ground cover, shovel, etc.) and was trucked to Firebase Birmingham, awaiting further orders. Since I was also trained on 81mm mortars, I spent a few days with a mortar team before being reassigned to a security unit at a nearby bridge the Navy SeaBees built crossing the Perfume River; it provided the only land access to two American Firebases. The Seabees also maintained a pumping station that provided non-potable water to the American headquarters at Phu Bai. The location was called Pohl Bridge.

Daily routines at Pohl Bridge included vehicular security checks as well as pulling all sampan river boat traffic over to check for contraband and proper ID's. At night we took turns on the compound perimeter and it was here that I earned my Combat Infantry Badge (awarded for being engaged with the enemy in a combat scenario). Our compound was nothing more than a sandbag perimeter with elevated fighting positions at each corner and a sandbag bunker that would sleep about six guys at a time. In the center of the compound we had an 81mm mortar pit. One side of the compound was pretty much open to the river. On the other side of the road (same side of the river) was a similar sized unit of South Vietnamese Army regulars (ARVN's). On the other side of the river was a small Seabee contingent.

About three days after arriving at Pohl Bridge, and within minutes of just coming off my guard duty and stripping down to my boxers to catch a few winks in the cot, all hell broke loose outside. We all had assigned fighting positions, and I grabbed my M16, my bandolier of ammo and I crawled out to my assigned position. That night I never fired my weapon and for the most part never looked over the top on my bunker assignment. I was petrified as the red and green tracers flew overhead and the sound of rounds hitting the sandbags sent me into a deeper crouch. The fight only lasted about 10 minutes. Nobody on our side was hurt, but I was a mess. No simulated training back in the States came close to preparing me for this, and when the dust had settled, my platoon sergeant, E7 Otero (nicknamed "Chief") came up to me and in a calm and soothing voice said "You didn't fire your weapon did you McAllister?" There was no lying to this man who was on his third tour in Nam; he knew what the answer was anyway. He put his arm around my shoulder and told me that he did the same his first firefight and that if I wanted to go home at the end of my tour, I would figure it out quickly. He also pointed out that your brothers here will expect you to pull your load and cover them. The next firefight came in two days and I was all in. Hard to believe I could transition so quickly from civilian life to war, but I wanted to make it home at the end of my tour, and I didn't want to ever let anyone down.

Occasional patrols from the compound into adjacent villages often flared into small skirmishes with the Viet Cong, and it didn't take long to become a seasoned "grunt."

About two months into my tour, the CO (Commanding Officer), a Captain Maratello came by and asked me if I would escort a couple prisoners back to Saigon, and when I was done with that, I was to report to Company Headquarters back in Phu Bai. I took the two VC down to Saigon on a Huey and returned to Phu Bai. There I was offered a job as a company clerk (they must have read my resume) and promoted to Specialist 4th Class. I thought this would be a good way to help my goal of getting home safely. However, the Army always has a way of throwing a monkey wrench into the mix.

A special recon squad was being put together to pull intelligence off high-speed infiltration trails (locations with high potential for enemy movement at night) and if necessary pull ambushes. I was asked to join the squad, promoted to Sergeant (E5) and off we went. Every afternoon we were briefed at Battalion headquarters and then inserted by helicopter at an LZ close to where we were to set up our observation/ambush. There were eight of us in the squad.

Small Viet Cong units would move from hamlet to hamlet at night, terrorizing the villagers into supporting their needs as opposed to supporting the Americans. Village allegiance would change daily, from American support during the day to VC support during the night. Our job was to observe and intercept where possible this nightly infiltration, and we got pretty good at it. But we all paid the price; two of our original eight were killed when we walked into an ambush and I took some shrapnel in the back from an RPG round that disintegrated a tree near me.

Somewhere in the middle of my tour, I needed something to offset living from firefight to firefight. So, when I had a few moments I sent a letter back to The Equitable and asked them if they would be willing to initiate a clothing drive for kids that could be distributed to one of the many orphanages that dotted the local villages. We named it "Project Smile." About two months later I got airlifted from our patrol back to the rear area where there were about 50 boxes of clothing that had been collected by my associates back home and shipped over by the Air Force. My CO made arrangements for a jeep and I distributed the clothes to the excited open arms of children who had been orphaned by the war. "Project Smile" brought many smiles that day to some who didn't have much of a reason to smile. It also put a smile on my face. For this effort and my service with the 101st Airborne unit, I was honored to be selected for inclusion in the 1971 volume of "Outstanding Young Men of America" published by the American Jaycees organization.

Back to the war. Six months later, in the name of Pacification, operations control halted the night maneuvers and we were integrated into the regular Recon Unit. After 10 months and 16 days in Vietnam, I was granted an early departure and left Cam Rahn Bay on December 25, 1970. It was a TWA "freedom" flight chartered by the military and when those wheels left the tarmac, there wasn't a dry eye on the plane. The flight attendants had Christmas cookies for us, and in all honesty, the transition was a bit overwhelming. From looking over your shoulder every minute to Christmas carols in a matter of hours is not an adjustment easily made. Some still haven't made it. Shortly before I left, the American squad at Pohl Bridge was discharged with security responsibility and the entire bridge was turned over to the ARVNs for control. When the American flag was lowered for the last time at the bridge, my CO gave me the flag for my service there. It is proudly displayed in my home today. Several months later, the bridge was blown up by the VC.

We returned to Fort Lewis where we took showers, were given new uniforms, given a steak dinner and paid. Next came the worst words I have ever heard, "If you have civilian clothes, wear those home because the public is spitting on soldiers returning from Vietnam." I made a conscientious decision to serve my country, and now, because the war is so unpopular in the States, I am reduced to something less than your average citizen. It was hard to accept and to understand, and it has taken some 45 years for that sentiment to be replaced with respect and admiration. Over 58,000 who paid the ultimate price for their service, along with thousands who have had to deal with PTSD and other combat related issues, never got to feel that respect. Troops from World War II were paraded and kissed by strangers in the street, Vietnam Vets were spit on and labeled baby killers, and the more recent Middle East Veterans seem to return to a more humane America. Maybe we have come full circle.

Over the past 30 some years, I have read and studied everything I could get my hands on about the history of Vietnam and our involvement, and watched all the documentaries and film footage available to understand what truly took place. In my humble opinion, we double crossed Ho Chi Minh when he sought U.S assistance to unite Vietnam, we supported a corrupt South Vietnamese government whose human rights agenda wasn't much better than that of the North, we had officials in our own government as well as military leaders in the field who fed falsified statistics to the American public to support a hawkish military buildup and presence, and worst of all, we did virtually nothing to support and assist our returning warriors to return to civilian life.

The people who protested in the streets and the musicians who sang about the turbulent times were frequently right in their discord; some very poignant notes were struck. Crosby, Stills, Nash and Young (Ohio); the Buffalo Springfield (For What It's Worth); Chicago (It Better End Soon); and Credence Clearwater Revival (Fortunate Son) were just a few that rang loud. My favorite while I was in Vietnam was We Gotta Get Out of This Place by The Animals. Every band that played for U.S. troops, whether Vietnamese or English, finished their set with this song.

I became a different person when I went to Vietnam. Whether that was for the better, you will have to ask someone who knew me before I went and after I came home. I am still proud to have served my country, regardless of the price I have paid. My only hope for those of you who read this is that you will never pass up an opportunity to say "THANKS" to a veteran.

During World War I, Ernest Hemingway volunteered to serve as an ambulance driver for the American Red Cross in Italy and was wounded by mortar shrapnel. While wounded, he assisted another wounded soldier for which the Italian government awarded him their Silver Medal of Valor. Much of Hemingway's writings reference war although most deal with the aftermath of war. His first two major novels, "The Sun Also Rises" and "A Farewell To Arms" are examples of these. In 1937 he travels to Spain to report on The Spanish Civil War which becomes the basis for one of his great novels, "For Whom The Bell

Tolls." During World War II while living in Cuba, he volunteers his fishing boat, "Pilar", to the Navy to look for German submarines in the Florida straits. While he never engaged one, he was awarded the Bronze Star in 1947 for his service.

American security outpost at Pohl Bridge,
I Corps, Republic of South Vietnam.

Getting ready for a perimeter patrol.

McAllister distributing "Project Smile" clothing to war orphans in South Vietnam.

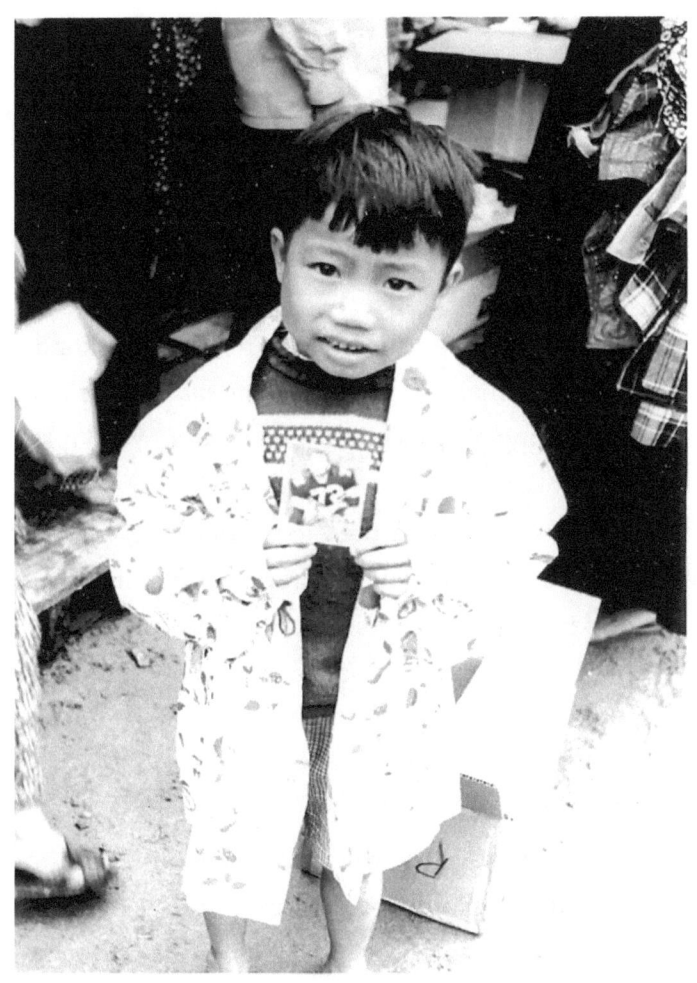

Getting a new shirt and a football bubblegum card.

Third Journey: The Florida Keys 1989

"Any man's life, told truly, is a novel."
Ernest Hemingway

You remember during my First Journey I had an epiphany after reading *The Old Man and the Sea* about someday having a connection with the sea. Well it happened.

After 17 years in the New York City corporate world, and a few more in Colorado Springs trying my hand at partnerships and small business ownerships, I purchased an interest in a scuba diving operation: Colorado Springs Scuba Center. In a short period of time I went from the basic Open Water Diver to an Instructor, and I really enjoyed the teaching aspect of the activity. What I didn't like were the cold water dive locations with no visibility that we were locked into. After taking a group of 35 customers on a dive trip to Islamorada in the Florida Keys, I came home with a clear vision of me relocating to the Keys and enjoying some of the most spectacular water anywhere until retirement, whenever that was to be.

I received an invitation to join the staff at Florida Keys Dive Center in Tavernier at the North end of Plantation Key, one of the four islands that make up Islamorada. So without much ado, I settled my affairs in Colorado Springs, jumped into my '62 Corvette, and began my next journey. I was single at the time, I liked Jimmy Buffett music, and spending all day on or under that beautiful water was not looking too shabby. Trading a three-piece suit for a bathing suit was a no-brainer.

Florida Keys Dive Center, affectionately known as "Flakeys", was founded and owned by Pam and Tom Timmerman. They ran two dive boats out of the store (The Little Dipper and the Goody II), and they were a 5-Star PADI facility (PADI at the time was the largest of the recognized scuba certification organizations) with a great customer base. Shortly after arriving, I was asked to manage the operation, but continued to teach all levels of dive certifications along with a staff of three other instructors. When we weren't teaching classes or working in the store, we would crew the morning, afternoon or night dive boats. It was the most fun I had had since counseling at a boys camp in Maine during my college summers. It didn't pay much but that was no longer a priority for me.

There were about 15 dive operations in the Upper Keys (Key Largo and Islamorada) at that time, and while we had little to do with the Key Largo operators, we all knew each other, assisted each other where we could, and socialized together on a regular basis. Guests who came diving with us, whether they were there for some level of certification or just for a two-tank dive trip to some of the best underwater sites in the United States, wanted to hang out with the dive shop staff to learn more about the "real Keys" they heard about in Jimmy Buffett songs and to see if they could get some of that "Keys disease" (I'll let you figure out what that's all about).

Within the first year, I purchased a house on the water (in Venetian Shores where we had boat access to the Atlantic and to the Florida Bay). Most dive instructors were a lot like ski instructors – just out of school and looking to spend a year or so having a good time while not making a penny. I was a little different, having completed a successful corporate career and arriving here with a decent financial base. I guess that's why most of the parties were at my house, and that was fine with me. I never flaunted my comfort level but it was hard to hide among the majority of troops who struggled to pay their rent. On top of this, all my friends from other parts of the states wanted to come to the Keys so my front door (and the door to the small apartment I had below my house) were always swinging open. More importantly, while I was no longer married, my daughter Lauren, who lived with her Mom in Michigan, spent every free day and summer with me. At least once a month without ever missing, I made a weekend trip to Michigan to be with her. I certified her at the age of 12 (the youngest for junior divers) and we ventured to other wonderful dive locations for our vacations (Maui, Cozumel, the Bahamas, Grand Cayman, Turks and Caicos, and St. Lucia).

Life in the Keys was fun back then. During the 13 years I lived there, I had a 36-foot Tiara sport fishing boat, a 25-foot Mako center console, and an 18.5 foot-Pro Line flats boat. There were more boats in Islamorada than registered cars and we did everything by boat: diving, fishing, cruising to the Sand Bar, bar hopping, dinner rides and sunset cruises. About the only thing we didn't do by boat was to make the periodic 86-mile trip to Key West and the ritual "Duval Crawl" (bar hopping on Duval Street). Strolling the streets of Key West and frequenting such bars as Sloppy Joe's, Ricks, Margaritaville, and Captain Tony's put you directly in the shadows of Ernest Hemingway, Jimmy Buffett, and many other piratical characters.

Life at the dive shop was a blast. A uniform consisted of flip flops, a bathing suit and a t-shirt; a perpetual tan, and a never-ending stream of fun and interesting people from all over the world. Being a single, "eligible bachelor," ensconced in this free-spirited world had its rewards as well. Filling tanks and cleaning the boats at the end of the day just whet our appetites for a rum runner at the "World Famous TIKI Bar" at the Holiday Isle Resort served by one of the all-time great bartenders, Trapper John, and maybe a conch fritter or two.

I was 44 when I arrived in the Keys and I wasn't running away from anything or trying to escape from anything, so that made me a little different from a lot of the transplanted "fresh water conchs" (natives born and raised in the Keys are called "Conchs;" people that move to the Keys and establish residency are referred to as "fresh water Conchs). Just about everyone in the dive business was from someplace else, but boy were there some characters. One of my boat captains claimed to not having paid for a dinner in five years, living off the happy hour "freebees" in the local hotels and watering holes. Another boat captain, originally from Australia, found a floating garbage bag full of $100 bills in the mangroves as he was heading to the morning dive site (about $100,000 was sent home to Australia for "future needs.") One of our temporary boat mates got arrested for exposing himself in the small local movie theater. We had a small boat ramp at our shop and it could only be used at high tide. One of our local "yocals" came in and obnoxiously demanded to use the ramp, even though it was low tide and obvious that there was not enough water to float his boat off the trailer. After listening to his tirade, I made him sign a release, warned him of the outcome, and sent him on his way. Ten minutes later, his Toyota pickup, the trailer and the boat all disappeared under water (the boat did pop up). He of course rushed into the shop demanding assistance. . .I handed him the phone and wished him good luck.

We had a good staff and we all enjoyed working together, even though the nature of the business threw challenges at us almost every day. Overseeing the safety of everyone in our charge was priority number one but there were always those hell-bent on pushing the envelope and ignoring our safety briefings. Beginning dive classes were divided into three parts; classroom work, confined water (pool) works, and four open water (in the ocean) check-out dives. Often, people would take their classroom and pool work at their home location and then take a referral form to a dive location located in a more tropical, vacation-like setting, like the Keys.

I got one such referral one day from a 65-year-old doctor. As I did with all referrals, I sat down with him and discussed how he did in his pool work, what concerns he had about doing the check-out dives in the ocean off the back of a decent size boat, and if there was anything else I should be aware of. They also have to complete a current medical questionnaire; in this case he answered everything negatively with no indication of any problems. On the way to the dive site, I again chatted with him and detected a little hesitation, but he said he was excited and good to go.

When we got to the first site, I got him into the water but that was about as far as it went. He couldn't get the floatation air out of his BC and he showed signs of panicking. I immediately got him out of the water and back onboard the boat, told him I would be back to work with him, and then took my other three students down for their checkouts. While underwater, I hear and see the bottom of a small boat approach, tie off to our boat, and then take off after five minutes or so. When I got back onboard, the mate said the doctor was complaining of being "bent" (Nitrogen narcosis which comes from breathing compressed air underwater for too long). In this case, the doctor never even got his face underwater so I knew it wasn't that – more likely some kind of a panic attack. When we got back to the dock, I found out that they took him immediately to the local hospital so I hustled off to see him. It turned out that the good doctor had a long history of congestive heart failure (which he not only failed to disclose to me but to his wife as well). He did apologize and said he would be back to finish his certification as soon as he got out. Really!!! I told him that I would notify the certifying organization (PADI) and have his name dropped from not only the referral list, but from ever being able to dive with an authorized agency. "Don't come back to my store!" I did contact his original certifying store and found out that he lied on their medical form as well.

This happened often, believe it or not. In many cases we don't find out about it until long after the certification is complete, and frequently over a couple celebratory drinks. As someone once said, there's no accounting for stupidity.

During my time teaching, I probably certified about 1,000 students – from the initial Open Water Class up through and including Divemaster. Being a teacher had always been in my DNA, but the pay differences between the corporate world and the education system drove me away from the classroom. Scuba diving gave me the chance to exercise that passion and I loved even the most challenging of students (except the good doctor).

In 1997 I decided to retire (diving was starting to take a small toll on my body) and spend more time fishing. I had a good friend who owned and captained an offshore sport fishing boat and he invited me to fish one of the local Sailfish tournaments. The second one we entered was Captain Al Fluties "Over The Hill" Sailfish Tournament and I took first place with 6 sails. I was earning my place as a respected billfish fisherman. The next year, we took his boat to Cuba for the Annual Hemingway Marlin Fishing Tournament, and didn't even get a strike. The following year we went over and I landed a 186-pound blue marlin although not big enough to place in the tournament (more on Cuba later).

Right around the same time, a gentleman who owned and operated a snorkel business in Key Largo contacted me to see if I would come out of retirement and help him expand his snorkel business to include diving, and open a significant dive retail business with it. While I really didn't want to get back into the fray, Danny Stahl was very persuasive and I joined "Sharkeys." We made the conversion and became a "player" in the Key Largo market. We went head-to-head with Spencer Slates' Atlantis Dive Center, Ocean Divers,

American Dive Center, and Quiescence, while still offering a snorkel-only adventure and ultimately a glass bottom-style reef trip. I returned to retirement after a couple years, but Danny and I remain best of friends to this day.

The Florida Keys have changed over the past 20 years. No longer those strange little islands that provided shelter to the middle-age runaways, no longer the open access to bales of drugs arriving daily, and no longer a secret about the quick escape from the real demands of everyday life. The money has arrived and it is very expensive to even sip a local margarita. One thing, however, has remained the same: the water. It still calls and answers to those who seek its redeeming and healing powers. Those same waters and spirits that called Hemingway in 1928 called to me in 1989. Hemingway lived there until 1939 although he owned his Key West house until 1961. I left in 2001.

Ernest and his wife at the time, Pauline, started renting a place in Key West in 1928 and then purchased his beautiful Key West home at 907 Whitehead Street in 1931. Unique to the house are the descendants of Hemingway's 6 and 7 toed cats who still roam the property today. In the relaxed life style of the Keys, including many days of fishing aboard "Pilar," he completed many of his most notable works, including "A Farewell To Arms" and "Death In The Afternoon." One of his favorite watering holes, "Sloppy Joe's," is perhaps the most popular of all the Key West bars.

Cruising Islamorada in my '62 Corvette.

A shark dive in the Bahamas.

Chasing bonefish on the flats of Islamorada.

Fourth Journey: Cuba 1999

"I have often wondered what I should do with the rest of my life and now I know – I shall try and reach Cuba."

Ernest Hemingway

Islamorada in the Florida Keys touts itself as the sport fishing capital of the world. If it's not it is certainly close. The best of all worlds: game fish offshore, bottom fishing on the reefs and wrecks, and world class shallow water fishing in the Florida Bay. At one time or another, I had boats to accommodate all three venues; a 36-foot sport fisherman to chase the sails and marlins, and a 28.5-foot skiff to pole the flats for tarpon, bonefish, and permit.

Fishing for me was more about time on the water. Everyone has their sanctuaries where you find peace from whatever stresses play against your head, your heart, and your soul. My sanctuary was on or under the water. Catching a fish was just icing on the cake, and after a while I was able to treat myself to some pretty nice goodies. I even caught some mahi, tarpon, and bonefish on a fly.

While doing some photography at the Holiday Isle Resort, I met and became friends with a young sport fishing captain named Greg Pope who owned and operated a boat named the *Tag'Em*. When special folks came to town and I wanted to show them an extra good time, we chartered the *Tag'Em* for a half or whole day trip. Greg was still earning his wings as a respected fishing captain among a fleet of famous and experienced guys and had worked his way up through the ranks before being able to buy his own boat. They respected him for his knowledge and for his commitment to run a respectable charter, even though he had yet to win his first tournament. His mate was Matt Grynawitz from Long Island. His dad was a Veteran and Matt's motto was "let's go kill some fish." I liked the guy. In 1998, Greg recommended that we try our hand at one of the annual Islamorada sailfish tournaments, the Al Flutie "Over The Hill" event (you had to be over 55 to fish in it). We signed up and I won the one-day event with six sails, twice having to handle two sails on at the same time (without any assistance from the crew). It was the boat's first tournament win as well as my first, and a strong bond was formed on that day.

Greg and I started chatting about the possibility of taking the boat to Cuba for the Hemingway Marlin Tournament, even though the U.S. embargo was still in place. Apparently, a number of the other boat captains had found a way to make the trip and not get themselves in trouble when returning through U.S. Customs. We decided to give it a try.

Greg was able to apply and receive a cruising permit from the State Department and we paid $50 for a letter from Club Nautico saying we would be their guest, all expenses covered, for the duration of our stay in Cuba. These two documents satisfied the government's concern that we would not be spending U.S. dollars while over there (more on that later) and that we had permission to take the *Tag'Em* over and back through controlled waters. So, on June 15, 1999 around 5 p.m., four of us, Captain Greg Pope, mate Matt Grenawitz, my good friend Danny Stahl, and myself took off from the Holiday Isle Marina bound for the Hemingway Marina about nine miles down the coast from Havana. We decided to make a night crossing so as to arrive at the marina check-in facility the next morning as the sun was coming up. The *Tag'Em* is a 55-foot custom hull vessel with a single Volvo diesel engine. Not the fastest sport fishing boat on the high seas, but one we were all comfortable with to be aboard. The night trip across the Florida Straits was really fun, although a little spooky. The sounds of the ocean (whales, dolphins, passing freighters, etc) in the dead black of the night (no moonlight that night) brought an eerie canopy over the boat as we chatted the night away and solved most of the world's problems.

When we arrived the next morning and made our way to the Cuban customs check-in point at the entrance to the marina, we were asked to vacate the boat while they inspected it. We were also advised that they were out of visitor's visas and that we would have to wait until they retrieved a new supply. As an accommodation to situations like this, there was a tiki bar adjacent to the facility, so we did what we thought everyone would do under those circumstances, drank some local rum.

Three hours later, the visas arrived and we were checked through customs and on our way to a dock in the marina (all of us with a little early morning buzz on). Waiting for us at our designated docking space was a young man named Ernesto who was to be our assigned dock assistant. Ernesto was 27 years old, a very nice, polite young man, who gave us the official lay of the land once we secured the boat. During our conversation with him, he asked where we planned to stay during our three-day visit. It was our intention to get a couple rooms there at the marina. However, Ernesto suggested that we consider staying at his mother and father's private residence in the small adjacent village of Jaimanitas (Hemingway frequently fished the *Pilar* out of this village) which they would rent to us for $50 for our entire stay (his parents would move out to a small out-building). Not only did we take him up on this offer, but we also asked Ernesto if he would show us around when we weren't out on the water. Cuban security measures would not permit Ernesto to join us on board while we were fishing.

That first trip to Cuba saw us skunked when it came to fishing, but it turned out that by far the best part of the trip was the opportunity to travel pretty much wherever we wanted to go with Ernesto as our guide and companion. We visited Hemingway's residence, *La Finca Vigia*, located near the small village of San Francisco de Paula in the hills overlooking Havana and where his famous boat "Pilar" is dry-docked and on display. We toured Havana, the old fort and made our way to two of the most famous bars in the world, The Floridita (home of the daiquiri) and La Bodeguita del Medio (home of the mojito). Someone said of La Bodeguita it is "a dive full of amiable scum, near the cathedral, where they serve mojito." I guess we fit right in. In 1953, *Esquire* magazine said of The Floridita, "an institution of integrity where man's spirits can be lifted by conversation and conviviality." Perhaps we were better suited for La Bodeguita. Hemingway frequented both.

The architecture in Havana is spectacularly diverse and eclectic. Perhaps most prominent is the Neoclassical and Baroque style, even more so than colonial Spanish. The problem is the economy. With very little of its national budget going toward infrastructure and building restoration, many of the classical buildings are close to collapse, or appear to be so. The cars are in a similar quandary; many great classic 50s and 60s American iconic models appear to be flashy and cool, but upon closer inspection, many of the bright colored paint jobs are spray-ons from a can and the engines are mostly Russian, European, or Japanese (the U.S. embargo has limited or restricted the availability of American products). We took a cab to dinner one night and were picked up by what appeared to be a very cool '55 Chevy. However, the only seat in the car was the one the driver was sitting on – the rest of us had to sit on the floor.

Ernesto took us out one evening to a local "disco" type facility adjacent to the marina, and sadly, it was packed with local young ladies selling themselves to anyone interested for small change. So sad for an economy that forces this upon you for basic survival. His girlfriend was a science teacher in the local high school and she made $27 dollars a week. We were, however, enjoying the local *Havana Club* rum in perhaps the most popular of the Cuban drinks, the Cuba Libre (coke and rum with a lime).

The last night of our stay, Ernesto's mom and dad had a picnic for us in their side yard and served local lobster and marlin, along with fresh vegetables and fruit. I am sure the cost of this special dinner was a setback for them, but we left a nice "thank you" tip before going home. We arrived not knowing a soul in Cuba, but left with a wonderful new friendship established with Ernesto and his family.

The trip home was uneventful and we were quickly cleared by a radio check-in with U.S. Customs. The next year the four of us went back again. Unfortunately, Ernesto's house was already rented out, so we stayed in the hotel in the marina. While we were there and relaxing in the on-site pool, we met the Cuban National Baseball team, and since I had some professional experience in the States, we bonded well with some of the players.

We brought with us from the States boxes of medical and bathroom supplies which we hoped to give to Ernesto and his family. Captain Greg's wife was a nurse at the Islamorada hospital and she was able to collect a nice variety of medical supplies whose shelf date had expired but were still very functional. Unfortunately, when we checked into Cuban Customs upon arrival, they found these items and confiscated most of them under the assumption that we brought them to sell on the black market. What they left us with we, did give to Ernesto and his family. Speaking of the black market in Cuba, there is a bit of irony here. There are two types of stores in Cuba: the peso store and the dollar store. The peso store is the legal store to shop in, but most have no or very little inventory. Virtually no customers either. The dollar store is the black market store and is based upon an illegal U.S. currency (illegal from an American standpoint but not for Cubans). These stores are full of inventory and bustling with business.

A note about the fishing this time. On day one of the tournament, I hooked and landed a 168-pound Blue Marlin. It took me about an hour to land this beautiful billfish, but unfortunately it wasn't big enough to place in the tournament. Unlike in America where we release all billfish caught (with the exception of swordfish), in Cuba marlin are kept and are a main part of their natural diet. We gave the fish to Ernesto and his parents who were extremely appreciative. Unfortunately, this practice is depleting the marlin fishery, and since they migrate through these waters on the way up the coast of the United States, it impacts our fishing as well.

My grandfather, Karl Weber (on my Mom's side) spent a year in Cuba with his brother after he graduated from McGill University in Montreal, Canada. They purchased some property on the Isle of Pines along the South shore of Cuba, and operated a grapefruit plantation. The government eventually confiscated the property, but I remember my grandfather telling wonderful stories about how much he loved the people and the land while he was there. I still have a cane that was hand-carved by the foreman of his farm. We found the same on our visits: the people were warm and hospitable and eager to chat. I hope to return again someday. In the meantime, I will continue to enjoy a Cuban rum drink now and then.

Ernest Hemingway got his first glimpse of Havana

when he was returning to Florida on the Steamship Orita in 1928. From Key West, many of his extended fishing expeditions took him through the "islands in the stream" and ultimately to trolling the deep canyons off the coast of Cuba. With the onset of Prohibition and The Great Depression, he found much more enjoyment in the rebellious bars and neighborhoods of Key West as well as other locations outside of the United States. With his love of fishing, of drinking and socializing with the locals and with those of note, it should come as no surprise that he would ultimately have a connection with Cuba. 1939 was a tumultuous year for Hemingway, particularly with the ongoing riff between he and Pauline. He shuttled back and forth between Key West and Havana and ultimately settled in Room 525 at The Ambos Mundos Hotel in Havana where he spent long hours working on his "For Whom The Bell Tolls" manuscript. With the assistance of Martha Gellhorn, he found a small house on a hill overlooking Havana called Finca Vigia, paid 18,500 pesos for it, and lived there for 20 years. As Hemingway became more reclusive at Finca Vigia, the influence of his writing became more pronounced, and life at this little house can be seen reflected in many of his works. He loved animals, but his favorite by far were cats and he had many at both his home in Cuba as well as his home in Key West. The descendants of his cats are still there today.

Ernest Hemingway lived a life defined by turmoil; it should then come as no surprise that the political and social turmoil found on the streets of Havana and the surrounding Cuban countryside would provide him with fodder for his life story.

Blue Marlin caught in the Hemingway Marlin Tournament in Cuba.

Amigos relaxing in Cuba; me, my friend Danny Stahl, Captain Greg Pope, and mate Matt Grynawitz.

Fifth Journey: Spain 2014

"Every man's life ends the same way. It is only the details of how he lived and how he died that distinguish one man from another."
Ernest Hemingway

Getting old is not for sissies. Looking backwards, I have always prided myself on staying active and staying in good shape. Never one to be a couch potato, I have enjoyed some wonderful and challenging activities; baseball, football, competitive swimming, competitive snow skiing, scuba diving, tournament fishing, distance running, camping, boating, and daily gym work. When one got boring or unavailable from a geographical or physical standpoint, I just picked another. I thought my life would continue this path until the end. Then in 2012, I got a wake-up call. In early July here in St. Augustine where I have lived since 2001, and while having dinner with my sister and brother-in-law who were visiting from the Atlanta area, I felt a little tightness in my chest. It went away in about 30 minutes, but returned the following evening for a little longer period of time. The next morning, while still feeling a slight tightness, I drove myself to the emergency room at our local hospital, and the rest as they say, is history. Two days later on July 12, I had a triple bypass open heart surgery to relieve two arteries that were 95 percent blocked and a third artery that was 75 percent blocked. While I had avoided the eminent heart attack, I was lucky to be alive. So for all the activity that I could put on my resume, the years of fast food and eating out regularly caught up with me and put some negative footnotes to it.

It was time to take stock and set in motion an updated plan that now, in addition to the regular exercise, included a dramatic change in my eating habits. I had to teach myself how to cook and how to eat healthy, non-fried and non-fat saturated foods. This is an ongoing challenge even to this day.

With strong recovery traits, I was back to starting a new exercise routine in 30 days that was predominately walking. It was relaxing and with my headphones to listen to my library of 60's music, I was up to four or five miles a day with no problem.

Then, while in Publix one day, I ran into an old friend of mine, Susan Harris, who was the Realtor who sold my house after my most recent divorce. Susan was a retired American Airlines pilot and she shared with me a trip she had recently made with a friend: a 500-mile walk across Northern Spain on a trail called the Camino de Santiago. She suggested I check it out as it might be "a walk" that I would really enjoy. She suggested I watch the movie "The Way" with Martin Sheen and his son, Emilio Estevez, which was about this journey. I did just that, and in all honesty, my life took on a new and somewhat cleansed perspective and renewed focus.

The Camino de Santiago is an ancient pilgrimage trail (actually a series of trails) that crosses Spain and ends at the town of Santiago de Compostela where the remains of the Apostle Saint James are said to be entombed. James is given credit for being the Apostle who delivered the message of Christianity to the Iberian Peninsula where paganism had been entrenched for hundreds of years. While there, he was called back to Jerusalem where in A.D. 44 he was beheaded and martyred. The story continues that two of his disciples took his remains on a boat journey back to Spain where he was ultimately laid to rest in what is now the cathedral in Santiago de Compostela. Thousands of pilgrims have been walking this trail, also known as the "way of St. James," since A.D. 850. During the Middle Ages, it was the leading pilgrimage trail in the world. Today, thousands of people from around the world make this journey, although not all do it for spiritual reasons. The most popular of these pilgrimage trails is the Camino Frances which starts in the small French town of Saint Jean Pied de Port on the French side of the Pyrenees Mountains and runs 500 miles across Northern Spain to Santiago de Compostela. This particular journey takes you through the Basque country and the town of Pamplona, the wine and olive country and the town of Burgos, the flat landscape of the Meseta and the old Roman town of Leon, and then through the province of Galicia and into Santiago. While I am a Christian, my time in a church has been limited over the past 40 years or so, but the thought of making this journey awoke some thoughts that had been dormant during that time.

The movie got me hooked, so I immediately started a new training regimen and studied everything I could find on the Camino. I attended lectures held by REI, I joined the American Pilgrims of the Camino organization, and I announced my intentions to my family and friends who thought I must have flipped my lid. Why would a 69 year-old man who recently had open heart surgery want to make a solitary 500-mile walking trip in a foreign land? Well, why not? My goal was to go the Spring of 2014 and I was not to be dissuaded.

I trained five days a week and built my walking distance up from four miles a day to 12 per day. About four months away from departure, I added my backpack and walking poles to the routine, constantly adding weight to the pack until I was comfortable with about 18 pounds (they recommend you carry no more than 10 percent of your body weight). I purchased and broke-in a great pair of Merrill hiking boots with Smart Wool socks, and felt confident that I had what I needed. John Brierly has written a guide to The Camino which breaks the 500-mile journey into 33 stages (days) and this would be my guide. It identifies starting and stopping points for each day, all the available albergues (pilgrim hostiles) and hotels along the way, water stops, places of interest and historical references. I would adjust as needed but my overall confidence was strong.

I decided to blog the entire trip since WIFI was readily available, and this would somewhat assuage my family and friends who were still skeptical about the wisdom of making this journey by allowing them to follow my progress, or lack thereof if there were problems. In spite of their skepticism, they gave me a variety of good luck charms and well wishes: my golf buddies Bob Broadbent and Dave Weitz gave me a plastic fork to hang on my backpack assuring me it would assist me with taking the right fork in the road; my sister gave me her pocket cross to carry; and my good friends Judy and Danny Stahl gave me a card with an Apache Blessing on it that goes like this: "May the sun bring you new energy by day, May the moon softly restore you by night, May the rain wash away your worries, May the breeze blow new strength into your being, May you walk gently through the world and know it's beauty all the days of your life." My friends Paul and Cathy Rayfield gave me a small silver bell that traditionally hangs on the bottom frame of your Harley motorcycle for a safe journey. I did have to mute the bell so that I didn't sound like a stray cow walking up behind people.

On March 31, 2014, I took an overnight flight to Madrid, arriving the morning of April 1. I caught the train to Pamplona and spent that night orienting myself to Spain and to the town that drew Hemingway further into his admiration for this country, having dinner at one of his favorite haunts, Café Iruna. It is here during the Fiesta de San Fermin where they run the bulls through the streets while crazy men in white outfits challenge these beasts to a game of chicken. Pamplona is on the

Camino so I knew I would be back. The next morning I took a taxi to St. Jean Pied de Port and registered with the official Pilgrim Office to acknowledge the start of my journey and to get the first stamp in my pilgrim passport (this is the credential that you carry and have stamped twice a day to acknowledge that you did in fact make the journey. In Santiago de Compostela, you present this stamped document to the Pilgrim Office there to receive your certificate of completion). I would start my 500-mile journey the next morning and I was excited.

  I awoke around 6:00am Thursday, April 3rd, had a brief breakfast in the albergue, and walked out into the street to begin my journey. It was dark and it was cold but my adrenalin was pushing me onward and ultimately upward. I knew these first two days would be the most demanding of the entire trip, climbing the Pyrenees Mountains on the French side and descending on the Spanish side. I had no idea what I was getting myself into and within the first hour, I was struggling. Struggling to the point where after the first two miles, I was having second thoughts about my sanity for considering this nightmare. I could turn around and walk back down into St. Jean, but I have never been one to quit or give up so easily. It took about six hours, but I made it part way up the mountain to the first albergue called Orrisson. This would be my refuge for the rest of that first day and night. It was quaint and cozy, the fireplace was roaring, the wine was flowing and the other arriving pilgrims seem to have made the same realization. On top of all this, it started to snow.

The albergues are usually dormitory style sleeping with community bath facilities, and it was here this first night that I met Roger Verlinden from Belgium. He and I shared a couple glasses of wine, talked into the early part of the evening, and ultimately walked together for a couple weeks. We have remained friends over the years. The next day we tackled the rest of the Pyrenees and made our way down into the Basque village of Roncesvalles, even though the mountain was covered in snow and a virtual white-out. Oops, I forgot to bring gloves. Needless to say, my blogs those first couple of days were not real inspiring to my readership and I'm sure more than a few expected to read about an accelerated flight home.

My plans were to walk between 12 and 15 miles a day, and with a few exceptions I was able to stick to that goal. In the small villages that dotted the entire journey, I would stay in the albergues and then when I arrived in one of the larger towns, I would treat myself to a private room in one of the more notable hotels. The first such treat was back in Pamplona (Day Six) where I stayed at the Hotel La Perla, another haunt of Mr. Hemingway. As a matter of fact, the room where he stayed and worked was turned in to a mini-museum. But the albergues are an integral part of The Camino and the experience. Dinners are served in a family style setting and usually consist of a homemade soup, a fresh salad, a meat or fish entrée with a couple fresh vegetables, and flan for dessert. Wine and beer accompany all the meals. Breakfast is usually a help yourself type setting with eggs, cereal, pastries, and fresh fruit available. The fresh squeezed orange juice is the best I have ever had. The dormitory style bedrooms are another story. For the most part, they consist of old-fashioned metal bunkbeds that creak loudly every time you move an inch. Add this noise to the coughing, the snoring, and the farts, and you have something less than the ideal sleeping conditions. But I didn't come here to sleep, so it was no big deal.

The next several days took us through the wine and olive groves. Roger and I made good time and we connected with a few other pilgrims, some of whom we met the first day of the journey at the Orrisson albergue in the Pyrenees Mountains. My legs were adjusting to the routine and my blogs actually got a little more positive and festive. It was not uncommon to separate from those you were walking with during the day; everyone's pace and stride was a little different but we would frequently meet back up at the end of the day's walk at the albergues. The solitude of walking alone in a strange land was as comforting as the companionship that seem to be always available.

Day 13 I walked into the town of Burgos and treated myself to another one of those upscale hotels, The Mason El Cid. Burgos is the home to one of the most beautiful cathedrals in the entire world, and I took an extra day to tour and enjoy its beauty. Construction of the Gothic style structure started in 1221 and it took over 300 years to complete even though restorations and additions have been never-ending. I was there for Palm Sunday and the pageantry was unlike anything I had ever seen.

A week later I walked into Leon on Easter Sunday but before I get into Leon, let me tell you about my favorite part of the journey: the Meseta. This is the flat, table-like landscape between Burgos and Leon that offers virtually nothing to look at other than this vast, vivid vista of green fields and farm roads. Many will tell you that this is the least favorite part of their walk. For me, it was by far my most favorite as I found the solitary

time in this nondescript zone the most spiritually inspiring. The early morning smells from the fields along with the chirping of the insects and birds soothed the senses and I was able to dial in an uncanny amount of clarity on many issues, some of which had been a mental burden for years. While I look back and relish all 500 miles of the journey, the Meseta defined my time on the trail.
Back to Leon. Founded as a military encampment around 29 B.C. by the Roman Legion, it is perhaps most famous as the first settlement in all of Europe to establish a parliament and a parliamentary rule of law. In addition, it has one of the most beautiful cathedrals in the world, renowned for an expansive collection of more than 120 stained glass windows. As I mentioned, I arrived in Leon on Easter Sunday, and for some reason, after eating all this fresh and healthy Spanish food, I craved an American hamburger, so I actually found a Burger King and had a Whopper as my Easter meal. What can I say!

From Leon, it took me another 15 days to walk to Santiago de Compostela. The last 5 days were in the Province of Galicia, beautiful rolling hillside country with vast Eucalyptus forests. But it rained every day. Once in Santiago, I did what every other pilgrim does: collapse in front of the cathedral giving thanks for having survived the ordeal. People dance, sing, drink or just stand there in a trance not completely sure about what really happened. At noon every day, there is a Pilgrim's Mass in the cathedral and it is packed for every service, and while the mass is delivered in Spanish, there is no doubt whatsoever about what message is being delivered and acknowledged.

The next day I took my Camino passport with all the stamps to the pilgrim's office and received my compostela (certificate). When asked by the office official why I made the journey, I said that I started the journey to make a statement of accomplishment, but along the way it took on a more spiritual endeavor.

Thirty-five days after starting my journey, I returned home. I was tired and my body needed a little rest, but at the same time, I have never felt more alive. I would make the 500-mile journey twice more in the following four years. As all pilgrims say to each other on the road, "Buen Camino."

On my third journey to The Camino in 2018, I traveled with Linda Simpson, and we did a side trip to the wonderful Basque seaside town of San Sebastian on the Northern Coast of Spain. This beautiful picturesque resort town offers some of the very best Basque cuisine known as pintxos. Similar to tapas, pintxos bars are everywhere and offer wonderful eating experiences. On this same trip, once we reached Santiago de Compostela, we took a day trip to Finisterra and to Muxia. Both are small historic towns located on the Atlantic coast and many believe that the Camino actually ends at these two sites.

By the way, I did not attend a bullfight.

———————————————

Shortly after the start of the Spanish Civil War in 1936, Ernest Hemingway went to Spain to cover and report on the war. Late in 1937 he wrote his only play, "The Fifth Column" while in Madrid with Martha Gellhorn who was to become his next wife. His fascination with Spanish bullfights and matadors provided the basis for some of his most popular works including "The Sun Also Rises." The majority of his time there seem to be between Madrid and Pamplona, both of which had large and popular bullfighting rings, "La Plaza de Toros." In "Death in the Afternoon," Hemingway explores bullfighting almost as a religion and compares it to a writer in search of the meaning of life. Later he would turn his opinion around and denounce bull-

fighting as a commercial and depressing spectacle. As for Spain, he told a friend that this is where he should have been born and the place of his spiritual rebirth.

Walking across the Pyrenees Mountains
on the Camino de Santiago in the snow.

My favorite part of the Camino, the vast, open Meseta.

Linda and I at the Cascada Ezaro Falls near Finisterre.

Epilogue

"It is good to have an end to journey toward;
but it is the journey that matters, in the end."
Ernest Hemingway

It was never my intention to imply that my life journeys were any more special than those of others. As Ernest Hemingway would have told you, they are just stories to be told. Like everyone else, I have been blessed with those special events and individuals that give me happiness every day: my daughter Lauren, my granddaughters McAllister and Lucy, and some very special friends who have been with me through thick and thin. So why this book? Well, perhaps Terry Pratchett said it best, "If you don't turn your life into a story, you just become a part of everyone else's story." Oprah Winfrey was pretty close as well when she said, "You define your own life. Don't let other people write your script."

I wanted to put mine down so my grandchildren and their children will have an idea of who their grandpa was. I am hoping that these notes will be some of the roots that help them bloom into full and beautiful lives, full of challenges and rewards for taking on those challenges.

The rewards for me have been "supercalifragilisticexpialidocious." Watch *Mary Poppins* one more time to reacquaint yourself with the joy that this nonsensical children's word expresses because that's just where I am. Thank you for taking these journeys with me.

Quotation Sources

First Journey: Vespa
"Every day is a new day."
> Ernest Hemingway: *The Old Man and the Sea*, 1952.

Second Journey: War
"Never think that war, no matter how necessary, no matter how justified, is not a crime. Ask the infantry and ask the dead."
> Ernest Hemingway: *For Whom the Bell Tolls*, 1940.

Third Journey:
The Florida Keys "Any man's life, truly told, is a novel."
> Ernest Hemingway:*Death in the Afternoon,* 1932.

Fourth Journey:
Cuba "I have often wondered what I should do with the rest of my life and now I know – I shall try to reach Cuba."
> Ernest Hemingway: Letter written to Pauline

Hemingway on or about March 28, 1928.

Fifth Journey: Spain

"Every man's life ends the same way. It is only the details of how he lived and how he died that distinguish one man from another."

> Ernest Hemingway: Documented in *The Good Life According to Hemingway*, by A. E. Hotchner, 2008.

Epilogue

"It is good to have an end to journey toward; but it is the journey that matters in the end." Ernest Hemingway (there is considerable debate that this quote is actually one by Ursula K. LeGuin).

Bibliography

Baker, Carlos. *Ernest Hemingway: A Life Story*. New York: Charles Scribner's Sons, 1969.

Brierly, John. *A Pilgrims Guide to the Camino de Santiago*. Scotland: Camino Guides, 2003.

Castro, Tony. *Looking For Hemingway*. Connecticut: Lyons Press, 2016.

Conrad, Winston. *Hemingway's France: Images of a Lost Generation*. California: Woodford Press, 2000.

Cortanze, Gerard de. *Hemingway in Cuba*. France: Editions du Chene, 1997.

Hemingway, Ernest. *The Old Man and the Sea*. New York: Charles Scribner's Sons, 1952.

Hemingway, Ernest. *The Sun Also Rises*. New

York: Charles Scribner's Sons, 1926.

Hemingway, Ernest. *Islands in the Stream*. New York: Charles Scribner's Sons, 1970.

Hemingway, Ernest. *Death in the Afternoon*. New York: Charles Scribner's Sons, 1932.

About the Author

Rick McAllister grew up in Cincinnati, Ohio, and in Severna Park, Maryland. After graduating from Susquehanna University in Selinsgrove, Pennsylvania, he spent two years in the United States Army, including a year in Vietnam with the 101st Airborne Division, and then 18 years with The Equitable Life Assurance Society in a variety of senior management positions. During his corporate career, he was selected for a year in the United States House of Representatives on a Congressional Assistant Program sponsored by the Brookings Institute.

In 1987 he moved to Islamorada in the Florida Keys and managed a scuba diving business for 12 years, including teaching scuba certifications as a Master Instructor. In 2001 he moved to St. Augustine where he resides today.

Rick is an active member of the St. Augustine Camera Club, and is a certified photo competition judge. His *Olde South Series* (over 500 black & white images depicting old abandoned and historic structures in the South) has been on display in a number of galleries and the subject of a number of publications. Rick is the author of *The Olde South: A Photo Journey Along the Back Roads of the South*, published in 2016. He also has been a feature writer for *Old City Life* magazine, as well as a few local newspapers.

www.ingramcontent.com/pod-product-compliance
Lightning Source LLC
Chambersburg PA
CBHW021119080526
44587CB00010B/575